T0065449

POETIC JOY

From Christian Echoes,
Echoes From Heaven,
The Listening Heart

MARIJAYNE

WESTBOW
PRESS®
A DIVISION OF THOMAS NELSON
& ZONDERVAN

WestBow Press books may be ordered through booksellers or by contacting:

WestBow Press
A Division of Thomas Nelson & Zondervan
1663 Liberty Drive
Bloomington, IN 47403
www.westbowpress.com
844-714-3454

ISBN: 978-1-9736-9700-8 (sc)
ISBN: 978-1-9736-9699-5 (e)

Print information available on the last page.

WestBow Press rev. date: 10/27/2020

There is joy in the heart of everyone
Who claim they love God's dear Son

And these things we write so that our
joy may be made complete. 1st John 1:4 NASB

MY STORY---GODS GLORY

I have always enjoyed writing poems. I have kept all those since I was twelve and in grade school. Which was the beginning of an enjoyable time working with words that rhyme.

From then until now I have many thoughts written, often on scraps of paper to catch the inspiration before it disappeared. However I now have them completed and collected them together to be put into my book titled "Christian Echoes" "Echoes from Heaven" and the "Listening Heart."

For those who have experienced the joy of writing and understand the satisfaction it brings, will agree with me, that writing is a gift from God. As I unwrap my gift for the readers, may they be blest by it, and perhaps become stronger in their faith.

All this reasoning makes it easy for me to praise Him and say, "To God be the Glory, great things He has done.

Sincerely in Christ,
Mary Jane Schuttinga
(Marijayne)

COULD I?

Could I take tomorrow- fresh and new-
And make it better than today?
So when it's gone into the past-
No loss be found along the way?

Could I leave a part of me
To help a fellow man?
Could I lift anothers' load-
With just a helping hand?

Could I make days brighter-
By willing tasks I've done?
So when I'm gone, I'll leave behind-
Lasting hope perhaps to one?

Could I?---with God's help, I'll try

Psalms 121:2 NASB *My help comes from the Lord, who made heaven and earth.*

THE LORD PROVIDES

When weary worn and tempted
For trials that come each day-
For needed strength to do our tasks-
The Lord provides the way.

The Lord provides the patience-
To carry burdens here-
He gives us strength and courage-
When life is filled with fear.

God provides our tomorrows-
With hope of future years-
He comforts when in sorrow-
And dries our flowing tears.

Our cross is sometimes heavy-
When loaded down with care-
He provides every need-
When we go to Him in pray,

Psalm 103:13,14 NKJV *Like as a Father pitys His children so the Lord pitys them that fear Him. For He knows our frame. He remembers we are dust.*

FISHERS OF MEN

Let down your net into the deep-
As Christ commands you to-
Launch out in faith upon the sea-
Where souls are needing you.

Let down your nets into the deep-
With love and try to win-
The multitude in darkness
Go fill and bring them in.

Let down your nets into the deep-
Of lifes' great sea of sin-
Where you are really needed
As fishermen of men.

Matthew 4:19 NASB *And He said unto them, "Follow Me and I will make you fishers of men.*

OUR ROAD MAP

The Bible is our road map as we travel here through life-
It shows the safest highways to avoid the way of strife.

The Kings highway is marked quite clear, follow at any cost.
Though the way seems narrow, if we obey we won't be lost.

We must study this road map-then
mark the road that is shown-
And check each time we stray, to find the way that leads home.

God made this road map long ago,
through His prophets I am told.
It will guide the young traveler on as well as when they're old.

It will guide us on the mountain top
or through the valley below-
Though we travel a lonely road, It gives assurance as we go.

Yes, the Bible is our roadmap. It was given to us by God-
It will lead us to eternal life, when
through heavens gate we trod.

Psalms 25:4 NKJV *Show me your ways,*
O Lord; teach me your paths.

SELF PITY

Self pity knocked at my door today-
and I quickly let it in.
So ready was I to have a good cry-
that I promptly let it begin,
Poking and proding, exposing my woes-
It brought them all into view.
Til' the end of the day, I was yielded to say-
What's the use, there's not much I can do.
When fear knocked at my door today-
I trembled with human care.
Faith and trust answered in its own knowing way-
When it opened, no one was there.

Hebrews 11:1 NKJV *Now Faith is the substance of things hoped*
for, the evidence of things not seen.

TRUST GOD

When a loved one hurts you, forgets and deserts you-
And love appears as a fraud-
When your heart is aching, until it's near breaking-
When life's at it's worst -------Trust God.

Trust God, He is there and always will care -
For He knows the path you have trod.
He'll go the last mile, whatever the trial--
His love is sufficient------Trust God

Psalms 118:8 NKJV *It's better to trust in the Lord than to put confidence in man.*

PEACE BE STILL

Storms of life rage 'round me, bringing tempest to my soul.
Oft time my hearts rebellion makes angry bellows roll.

Jesus knows my storm of life, when I fight against His will-
In a quiet small voice of comfort, He whispers,
"Peace be still." **Mark 4:39 NKJV**

These things I have spoken unto you that you might have peace.
In the world you shall have tribulation; but be of good cheer, I
have overcome the world. **John 16:33 NKJV**

DEVIL BEWARE

Devil - You get out of here you're standing in my way.
I don't have time to listen now-I have a busy day.
I can't stop now and listen-to the things you're talking of-
Don't tempt me with your foolishness, I've orders from above.
Don't whisper soft and coax me, to lie, to cheat and hoard-
Just get yourself away from me, I'm working for the Lord

James 4:7b NASB *Resist the devil and he will flee from you.*

WHY SURE

What makes the snow sparkle on a sunny day?
Where does the white go when it all melts away?

Where does the wind rest long before it blows?
Why can't we see it except where it goes?

How can the bee fly with no motor at all?
Carrying its body with wings frail and small.

What pushes the flowers when they're ready to grow?
In all of these matters, I would like to know.

Where does the light go when the dark comes along?
Where is the music when there is no song?

How can a red cow eat grass that is green?
Then give us white milk so good, pure and clean.

What holds up the rain when the clouds combine?
Where is the twinkle when the stars don't shine?

Where does the day go when tomorrows come?
Where are the memories before we had some?

How old is God and what is His size?
Someday He'll tell me and what a surprize!

In all of my wonderings, I'll wonder no more-
He'll give me the answer and I'll shout----Why sure!

Psalms 72:18 NASB *Blessed be the Lord, the God of Isreal, who alone works wonders.*

ONE LIFE-ONE SOUL- ONE LORD

One life I have for me to give-for selfish gain or freely give-
To help someone who has much less -or
search for true happiness.

One soul I have-I must beware-to always trust it to Gods care.
For He alone can keep it true- to live the life He wants me to.

One Lord to watch and care for me- for
from my sin He set me free
So I could give one life-one soul- surrendered all to his control.

Ephesians 4:6 NASB *One God. Father of all, who is above all*
and through all and in you all.

WATCH IT!

You say you are a Christian- your heart to the Lord you give-
Be careful what you say or do-folks are watching how you live.

You've told them about your titheing-
and how they should give-
No use wasting words for after all-
they're watching how you live.

Words are useless by themselves-and empty as a sieve-
You may be their only Bible-and they' watching how you live.

You've tried to be a witness- the gospel to them you give-
It really doesn't do much good-if you're
not watching how you live.

What you do speaks so loud- that what you say---I'm positive-
Will not be heard-for all the while-
they're watching how you live.

Matthew 15:8 NKJV *This people draw nigh unto me with*
their mouth, and honors me with their lips, but their heart is
far from me.

PREACHER STEW

The other day I stopped a while -as I was going out of church.
I heard a group of good folk say, it's time we make a search.

For a man who will stand and preach-
and tell it from the Bible.
Instead of fooling time away-get someone more reliable.

To tell us about our do's and don'ts-
remind us when we're wrong-
At least get one that carrys a tune-and can lead us with a song.

I walked on then out of church- and thought a little while--
Of another group the week before- and
it almost made me smile-

For then he preached so very strong-of
judgement, Hell and fire-
Some folks squirmed around to say-He should be up for hire!

We've got to get him out of here He's causing too much smoke-
He's scaring all the little ones-his way is just no joke.

How can a preacher satisfy-what can the poor man do?
I heard a bit of wisdom- so I'll pass it on to you.

Get on your knees and humbly pray- for
God to see him through-
The many times he's criticised- as good folks often do.

Then pray for our own weakness- I'm sure we need it too.
Next Sunday have some humble pie-instead of preacher stew.

James 5:16a NASB *Confess your faults one to another and pray*
for one another.

BACK'ACHE

When the day seems dark and gloomy,
though the sun is shining bright-
When I feel things going badly
and nothing is quite right-
When I am tempted to do wrong
and my burden's a heavy pack-
It's then I start to realize,
the devils on my back!

When I am weighted down so low,
that gloom is all around-
Self pity is working overtime,
that it almost gets me down-
I drag my feet as I walk along
and troubles begin to stack-
Again- I need to realize-
the devils on my back!

So then I get my Bible
and read of His love for me-
How He took all my sin away
when He died on Calvary.
He tells me He will give me strength
when my faith has been so slack-
For it seems my faith gets very weak
when the devils on my back!

So in His word I find relief-
and with new strength I find-
My troubles seem to fade away-
leaving hope and peace of mind.
The day is so much brighter
and for all the things I lack-
The Lord is there to help when the devils on my back!

Submit therefore to God-resist the devil; and he will flee from you.
James 4:7 NASB

MY SEARCH FOR PEACE

I searched for peace in the valley-
it was there for just a short while.
The mountains then seemed so inviting-
but alas it ended in trial.

I searched for peace in quiet places-
by rivers and streams hard to find-
But the turmoil I had deep within me-
continued to whirl in my mind.

I searched for peace in pleasures-
of friendships and good times galore-
I took what the world had to offer-
then began my searching once more.

I searched for peace with soft music-
melodies of song soothed my soul.
But soon the harmony ended-
leaving worry and grief in control.

Then I looked for peace in the Bible-
with a troubled heart I cried-
Lord, give me the peace I am needing-
peace which the world has denied.

He said, "My peace I will give you-
if you'll ask, confess and receive-
I am the way, the truth- and a life of peace-
when you trust Me and believe.

The peace of God which surpasses all comprehension
shall guard your hearts and your minds in Christ Jesus.

Philippians 4:7 NASB

REAL LOVE

Love is such a busy word- Who can know what it's all about?
Who can tell what love really is--
it's so quiet and yet it's a shout.

They say, Love makes the world go
around- also that love is blind.
Love can be a sacred thing-and a precious joy to find.

When marriage vows are spoken- and two hearts beat as one-
Who doubts the lovelight in their eyes-I'm sure there are none.

God gives the love that marriage has--—until death they do part
He asks them -to honor that love- and
keep it close to their heart

Who can explain a Mother's love- as
she holds her children tight.
Her love protects that little one- and
calms their cry in the night.

Jesus knows why a Mother loves - in
spite of a child doing wrong
The love He gives her through the years -helps
her love to remain strong

Who knows what love really is-the kind that is strong and true?
Jesus knew for the price He paid-to go to the cross for you.

Since love makes the world go around-
you must believe it's true.
For He holds the world in His mighty
hand- and controls it's actions too.

Love is blind? it surely must be -for at
the cross He covered my sin.
Because of His love he sees them no more-no
matter how sinful I've been.

Why does He wait so long for each one- as
he tenderly looks from above?
The Bible tells in a knowing way- it's
because of His wonderful love.

1 John 3:1 NKJV *Behold what manner of love the Father has bestowed upon us that we should be called the children of God.*

MY SHEPHERD
(Poetic Paraphrase of the 23 Psalm)

The Lord is my Shepherd, I shall not want-
nor shall I have need for more,
He makes me lie down in green pastures-
to rest when my labor's are o'er.

He leads me beside the still waters-
to satisfy my thirst and then-
He restores my soul with gladness-
and makes my heart sing again.

He leads me in paths of righteousness-
For His name sake I'll follow Him there-
Even though I walk through the shadow of death-
I'll feel safe for I know He does care.

I will fear no evil-for He is with me-
no harm will befall me I know-
His rod and his staff they comfort me-
and will guide me wherever I go.

He's prepared a table before me- I am filled,
and with new strength I find-
In the present of my enemies I fear not-
His protection will always be mine.

He anoints my head with oil of compassion-
He's chosen me as His precious one-
My cup runs over with gladness-
and His blessings have only begun.

Surely goodness and mercy will follow me-
all the days of my life and then-
I will dwell in the house of my Lord forever-
With Jesus- my Master and friend.

Psalms 27:1 NKJV *The Lord is the light of*
my salvation, and whom shall I fear?

The Lord is the strength of my life, of whom shall I be afraid?

JUDGEMENT DAY

*(Today Christ can be your Savior, but there will
come a time when He will be your Judge)*

GUILTY!---*the Judge thundered as the gavel came down.*
GUILTY?--- *from my throat came the rasping sound.*
GUILTY?---*NOT ME! and I wept in despair.*
How can this be, for I was not there?
How can you say ---that I am guilty today?

*I did not cause your back to be torn,
by thirty nine stripes given in scorn!
I did not put those thorns on your head-
-nor say those hateful words that were said!*

CRUCIFY----CRUCIFY--*was **their** cry!*
NO! *I did not cause a good man to die!*

*I did not mock or spit in your face-
nor cause you to die the death of disgrace,
I did not hammer those spikes in your feet-
and let you hang there in hopeless defeat.
Somebody else nailed your hands to the tree-
Somebody else--but it sure wasn't me!
You as my judge can surely see-
I did not cause you to hang on that tree!
I've been a good person, You know that is true-
And I've tried my best to live right for you.
I plead on your mercy, to review my case-
Please, don't sentence me--to that awful place!*

The gavel resounded, and the Judge spoke again-
I've rechecked your records and I find only sin.
Yes, You tried to be good with self righteous behavior-
But you rejected me as your Lord and Savior..
I died so your sins could be taken away-
and to keep you from facing this last judgement day.
Yes, you crucified me-though you were not there-
Your rejection of me is the guilt you must bare.
Your sentence is sure———forever in Hell——— you will be-
I never knew you——— depart now from me!

Matthew 7:23a NASB *And I will declare to them, I never knew you-depart now from me*

A PROMISE IS A PROMISE—
AND SO ARE EXCUSES

Lord, I'll give you an hour on Sunday- even
smile if the preacher is funny-
I'll clap if the music is stirring- but
please don't ask for my money!

I'll shake the hand of the visitors-and
welcome them all with a smile.
But the offering plate makes me nervous-
when the ushers pass by in the isle.

You said, to give as we prosper-and bring
to the storehouse each week.
But the lottery took my last dollar-that I
got from my last winning streak.

My insurance is due this Friday-and
the loan at the bank is too-
For the new car I bought last winter-so
there isn't much left for you!

But I sure won't forget the missions-I'll
bring the old clothes I can't wear-
My garage sale had plenty left over-I
do want to show that I care.

If I had oodles of money-Plenty of time with nothing to do-
I would help you out more often- to
prove how much I love you.

I'm really not making excuses,-you know I'd give if I could.
And I'd even try to give extra-Truly, I honestly would!

Let each one do just as he has purposed
in his heart- not grudgingly
or under compulshon- for God loves a cheerful
*giver. **2nd Corinth. 9:7 NASB***

SEND ME

Where is the one who would labor for thee?
Willing to go; where can they be
The harvest is ready; the laborers are few-
No one seems willing His work to do.
Where is the one who is willing to go?
To gather the harvest before winter's snow.
God needs laborers, where can they be?
Could it be you, could it be me?
Am I the one to answer the call
Are you the one to give of your all?
Could you and I answer the masters plea
With here I am Lord, Please send me.

So as much as in me. I am ready to preach the Gospel. **Romans 1:15a NASB**

THE CRUCIFIED CROOK

Gasping for air as he hung in space,
suffering the horrible death of disgrace-
Nailed to a cross on Calvary's hill——
knowing he deserved this old rugged place.

Rebuking the thief on the other side-
he said, our guilt cannot be denied.
But this man in the middle has no sin,
then he begged for forgiveness and cried-

Remember me Lord, this is my plea--
from all of my guilt-I want to be free.
With a heart of compassion, Jesus said,
today in Paradise-you'll be with me.

Forgiveness was granted for Jesus took-
all his sins from the masters book.
Eternal life was promised with much more-
to a redeemed soul, the crucified crook.

Titus 3:7 NASB *That being justified by His grace we might be made heirs according to the hope of eternal life.*

GOD SAYS-

Keep your eyes on Me, my child- be aware of where your walk.
Don't let Satan trip you up-don't listen to his talk.

I'll work within your life, my child-If you will keep Me there-
If you should fall, I'll catch you-and keep you in My care.

If you will wait upon me, my child- I'll teach you how to run.
You never will get weary--when you pray-"Thy will be done"

I will let you soar my child – with eagles wings on high-
Some day- right into my heaven --somewhere beyond the sky.

Isaiah 40:31 KJV *But they that wait upon the Lord shall renew their strength They shall mount upwith wings as eagles; they shall run and not be weary; and they shall walk and not faint.*

GIFTS

What did you get for Christmas, is the question often asked
Was it just what you needed, or more things that do not last?

What was your need this Christmas,
did you get your hearts desire?
Or was it like the wrappings, soon
crumpled and tossed in the fire?

What did you give for Christmas, do you think it was enough?
To bring them joy and happiness, or just more of useless stuff.

What God gave us for Christmas so many years ago-
Was a baby in a manger for all the world to know.

The best of earthly treasures was sent from heaven above-
Wrapped in a tiny package was the gift of Gods great love.

A gift that knows no measure and only will enhance--
The beauty of forgiveness - with knowledge of another chance

So take this gift he offers you- receive it now without delay
For Jesus is the reason- that we celebrate Christmas day.

For what you get from Jesus will always be enough
He gives an everlasting gift- instead of useless stuff

James 1:17 NASB *Every good thing bestowed and every perfect gift is from above, coming down from the Father of lights with whom there is no variation or shifting shadow.*

LIFE GOES ON

When death has come and tears do fall-
for a loved one here whom God did call-
When my Lord took my loved one home-
To dwell with him to no more roam,
My life must still go on,
Though grief has brought my spirit low-
Those who share my grief also know-
Sympathy of friends soon fade away-
For they don't feel the loss each day-
True, Their life must still go on.
God left me here to carry on-
I'll trust his love to lean upon
My task here is not finished yet-
I'll live for Him and not regret-
That my life must still go on
Yet, when he beckons and shadows fall-
and I must answer to His call-
I know I'll see my loved ones face
In that fair land there is a place-
For our life to still go on.

1 Corinthians 15:55 NKJV *O death where is your sting?*
O grave where is your victory?

WRINKLES

Today I looked into the mirror- and smiled back at myself.
I saw those wrinkles mocking me- like some mischieveous elf.

I do not like to look as if- I'm related to a prune-
Old age has surly caught me- and it came so very soon.

Although I know I'm ageing- young at heart is my goal.
With God's help I'm trying- to keep the wrinkles from my soul.

Psalms 37:25 NASB *I have been young and now I am old.*
Yet, I have not seen the righteous forsaken.

JUST SUPPOSE

God could have created Jesus- like He did Adam and Eve
But He wanted to send a baby- He chose Mary to conceive.

But suppose Mary had refused- to bear her little one-
After all-she wasn't married-and she was so very young.

She'd be so embarrassed- that others soon would know-
What would all the neighbors think- when she began to show!

And how about her boyfriend Joseph-who knew it wasn't his-
He could have said, "it's not mine-I
don't care if this child lives!"

Besides, babies take too much time, there's things I want to do-
I'm not ready to be a father, this just can not be true!

Just as Christ was sent through Mary-by means of natural birth
Babies are special messengers that God sends down to earth.

No matter how they were conceived, He sends them anyway-
To be a blessing to the world, if they're allowed to stay.

God hears the painful cry of millions-of those denied their life-
He sees the struggle in the womb-as
they're silenced with the knife!

He knows how great they could be-as a warrior for His cause-
But the battle is lost before their birth
by favored pre-choice laws.

God loves those precious little ones-
even though they're born in sin-
He gives them life for others to see-
and perhaps their soul to win.

Yes, God chose that time in history-
salvation He wanted to give-
Praise God for Mary and Joseph who
allowed their child to live.

And they came in haste and found their
way to Mary and Joseph
and the baby as He lay in the manger. ***Luke 2:16 NASB***

THE DOOR TO A NEW YEAR

I stand at the door of this new year-
I hesitate to turn the key.
What does this year have in store-
what will be there for me?

The time ahead I cannot see-
there's so much I do not know-
For days must be what they must be-
God planned it long ago.

I'll open the door to this new year-
knowing I must enter in.
To face the days and weeks unknown-
that are destined to begin.

I'll pause on the threshold of the new-
looking back with a sigh and tear-
To see that time has quickly closed-
the door to a passing year.

As I walk through the door of this new year-
uncertain of coming fate-

No matter what each day may bring-
I pray it will be great!

Hear my son and accept my sayings-
and the years of your life will be many.
Proverbs 4:10 NASB

THEY CALL IT MUSIC

Some people claim-that hymns are the best-
for sacred churches who care-
True- many found God through the anthems of faith-
as their songs flowed through the air.
They say there is truth- in those faithful hymns-
of Fanny Crosby, Wesley and more-
We are the results of the words they wrote
by the saints who lived here before.

There's Blue Grass country gospel-Wal ya al' gotta know-
has a twit and a twang all it's own.
Many quartettes harmonize through their nose-
as they sing of heavens bright home.

Yes, Negro spirituals and southern folk songs-
with it's mourning cry when they falter-
As they sang "Swing Low" and I'm Coming Home-
has brought many lost souls to the alter.

Contemporary is fine-if you're liking that kind-
The message is there-you must know-
Though it is different in so many ways-
your liking for it just might grow.

Gospel Rock? Well, what do you know
It's fast-loud with a hammered beat-
When you first hear it you must be aware-
It may knock the socks off your feet.

But there is a message in there- somewhere
If your heart and soul are in tune.
It just depends what age you are in-
Perhaps you were born much too soon!

However---some music drones -with the devils beat-
so loud- it about cracks your ear-
The soul is not blessed by the words they say-
Cause-you're not sure-what you hear.

I wonder if God is pleased with the noise-
that is claimed to be music in song-
Perhaps He's up there plugging His ears-
because all the motives are wrong.

Do we sing with love and joy in our heart?
With a message that must be told-
Are we listening with that same reason too -
Could it be our hearts have grown cold?

Whatever we choose-in this vast music world-
Our God must be in control.
For the music that is- the best for us all-
will honor His name-and bless our soul.

Sing for joy in the Lord, O you righteous ones. **Psalms 33:1 NASB**
Sing to Him a new song; play skillfully with a shout of joy.
Psalms 33:3 NASB

ECHOES FROM HEAVEN
BY
MARIJAYNE

Words that would soften grief–
if we could hear from our loved
ones who have just passed away.

ECHOES FROM HEAVEN
(written when my daughter had a miscarriage)

I'M OKAY MOM

God put me in the cradle of your body for a while.
Though I was just beginning-I know I made you smile.

He gave me to your keeping-from His heavenly home above-
As you rocked me in your cradle-I could feel your mother love.

I wanted to stay longer-til' the day of birth and after-
To grow up with my family- with all it's joy and laughter.

I'm sorry that because of me- your dear hearts have to ache-
But God in all his wisdom-never does make a mistake.

He knows that you are hurting and also wondering why-
He told me all the reasons-so Mom, please don't you cry.

I really am okay Mom-and life up here is grand-
I now am made so perfect-completed by Gods hand.

DO NOT WEEP
(written when my sister died)

Do not stand at my grave and weep-
for I am not there-nor do I sleep.
I'm enjoying my home God prepared for me-
I now am made whole and my spirit is free.
From the body I lived in- made of clay-
That imprisoned my soul and was wasting away.
To all my love ones-family and friends-
Do not be sad because this life ends.
Enjoy the memories of my life with you-
The good times with laughter and some sorrow too.
Children, I know there were times that were bad-
As we struggled together with out your Dad.
Often I wondered just what I should do-
But now we're together waiting for you.
Please, don't miss heaven-faith in Christ is the key-
We'll then be a family-the way it should be.

DEAR MOM AND DAD
(A teenager's death from a car crash)

While you're looking through a darkened glass-
wondering why I had to die-
I'm looking in the face of God
and He told the reason why.

Though my earthly life has ended-
My pain has ceased to be-
My life here is so much better-
I have peace and now I'm free.

Free from my many troubles-
that I battled there on earth-
And now I know the reason why-
You were chosen- to give me birth.

God knew I needed someone-
who would love me as I am-
He knew that you were special-
and would always understand

I have met my little brother-
who came here-so long ago-
I've told him all about you-
I thought you'd like to know.

We both are waiting for you here-
of course we don't know when-
Since good-bys are never easy-
We'll just say, "So long" until then.

GOD HAD A REASON
(written after the death of a friend)

God had a reason that I should go-
when I wanted so much to stay.
To live my life longer-with family and friends-
but God didn't plan it that way.

God had a reason- for letting me know-
that my life on earth would soon cease.
I could have gone sooner-a few months ago-
but he gave me a chance to find peace.

God had a reason for tears that you shed-
perhaps to get close to your heart-
For often in grief -we'll reach out to Him-
When friends and loved ones must part.

God had a reason-though death seems so hard-
to you who grieve for my sake-
Have faith -that this is all in His will-
for He never does make a mistake.

AFTER DEATH-WHAT THEN

(written when my Mom died)

When you look upon my face
-so free from earthly care -
Weep not for me and what remains-
the form that's lying there.
My real self is with the Lord-
I've peace and joy sublime-
Don't grieve why death has come-
He'll reveal it in His time.
Rejoice with me-my soul has gone-
from my body made of clay-
Weep not for me -it won't be long-
you too must go this way.
So think about your time to die-
will I meet you all again?
Will it be at Heaven's door?
If you should die-what then?

A NOTE FROM HEAVEN
(a sad farewell)

Seems life had gone by so quickly. I can
not count the times I've said-
There's plenty time to work for Jesus- now
my life's over and I'm dead!

Dead? No, not really-here in heaven my soul is living still-
Now I wish I'd been more faithful-seeking out my Fathers will.

Busy? Yes, that was my excuse- for having no time to do-
Daily prayers and Bible reading- or
tell others that He loves you

Saved? Yes, I knew the Savior-as a child I told Him so-
But I used my time for selfishness - til'
He said, "it's time to go."

Sorry? Yes, I'm very sorry that I didn't count the cost.
Wasteing time on earthly pleasures, now I only count the loss.

Will you take the time my dear ones-
while you have the chance today-
Do not wait until tomorrow-for they quickly fly away.

There are friends who need the Savior-
their life may soon be past.
Don't be foolish in your choices-time goes by so very fast.

MY JOURNEY TO HEAVEN
(Written when my brother died)

So many roads I have traveled -
many valleys and mountains I've climbed.
Jesus was with me each step of the way-
no better friend could I find.
Quickly my days have all slipped away-
leaving memories of much joy and tears-
My time on earth seemed very short-
as the days grew fast into years,
The last road I traveled-I wasn't alone-
I knew you were praying for me.
Jesus walked beside me-tenderly holding my hand.
Makeing the journey- safe as can be.
Are valleys and mountains now in your life?
Are you trying to go there alone?
Let Jesus my friend-keep walking with you-
As He did for me- to this heavenly home.

A YOUNG MANS FAREWELL
(written when my nephew died of cancer)

*My stay on earth has not been long- I
was scarcely becoming a man.
My purpose on earth is now fulfilled-I
am part of Gods sovereign plan.
He used my life in a loving way-though
suffering was all you could see.
Enduring the pain each day by day- He
became more precious to me.
Friends as you came here to say good-
by-to this worn out body of clay-
I only regret my death makes you cry-
that I should leave you this way,
Dad don't worry that life here is done.
In heaven I'm living with joy.
And Mom don't cry for your youngest son
cause God is here with your boy.*

GOD'S AMAZING GRACE
(written after a friends miscarriage)

I'm sorry I had to say good-by---before I could say hello-
I didn't mean to make you cry-but God chose me to go.
Back to His gentle loving arms-where he holds me oh so tight-
Don't worry about your little boy cause I'm safe and doing alright,
So Mommy and Daddy-please don't cry-
I'm sorry that I caused you pain
Don't feel guilty and wonder why-for sure you are not to blame.
Be ready to meet me in heaven for God is preparing a place.
We'll spend eternity together-all because
of God's amazing grace

IT'S ONLY BEGUN
(my parting farewell)

The end has not come-it's only begun.
Though death has closed this life's door.
I'm leaving behind this body of mine-
For a new one with blessings galore.

The years God gave-truly were blessed.
Though I also had sorrow and pain-
But in His loving way-the start of each day-
Held the promise of beginning again.

Earth's future tomorrows -I'll no longer see.
Heavens home is now in full view.
My body's at rest-I'm enjoying the best-
I'll be watching for you to come too.

No, the end has not come-I've only begun-
To enjoy what God promised me.
So don't shed a tear-for I'm happy here.
With Jesus- whom I've longed to see.

POETIC PRAYERS FOR THE LISTENING HEART
BY
MARIJAYNE

Lord, Grant me the wisdom to impart.
Not only a listening ear but a listening heart.

Search me O God and know my heart.
Try me and know my anxious thoughts.
Psalm 139:23 NASB

MY MORNING PRAYER

Good Morning Lord, Its good to know-
you've kept me through the night.
Just knowing that you care for me-
makes this new day start right.
I've got such a busy day Lord -
with many things to do-
But first, let me thank you Lord-
for watching all night through.
This day is such a pretty day-
I can see the sun will shine.
And even if the clouds do come-
It's bound to be just fine-
If you will walk along side me-
in everything I must do-
And guide me so I'll do my best-
so I can bring honor to you.
I read in your word today-
this is what you said to me-
If I would just obey and trust-
a better soul I would be.
Now Lord- You know I'm trusting you-
and I'm trying to obey-
So I can claim when evening comes-
it's been a perfect day.

Do give me strength when tempted-
to keep me free from sin-
And guide me through another day-
for Jesus sake––Amen.

My voice shall you hear in the morning, O Lord-in the
morning will I direct my prayer unto thee and look up.
Psalms 5:3 NKJV

MY TALK WITH GOD

Here I am again Lord. I need your help some more.
I'll beg your forgiveness since I bothered you before.

I have another problem, Lord-It's one "I'm sure you know
But telling you about it-does help my spirit so.

Thank you Lord for listening and helping once again-
I feel so much better now- since I talked with you-Amen

Let my cry come near before you, O Lord.
Psalms 119:169a NASB

THE SINNERS PRAYER

Though your list be long in prayer-
the needs of others asked with care.
When trials you bring for God to see-
Please take time to pray for me.
When you pray for health and more-
for a precious one whom you adore-
When you plead on bended knee-
will you please remember me.
There's so much fear I have within-
my eyes are blind to all my sin-
Ask the Lord that soon I'll see-
When you pray, please pray for me.

The troubles of my heart are enlarged. O bring me
out of my distresses. ***Psalms 25:17 NASB***

MEAL TIME PRAYER

Heavenly Father we thank you -as we gather around this food.
For your bountiful love before us- from
your hand so kind and good.
Bless this food dear Father-as we partake it to ourself-
May it give us strength today- and keep us in good health.

Blessed be the Lord who daily loads us with
benefits. **Psalms 68:19 NKJV**

EVENING PRAYER

Thank you Lord for strength you gave-
to face my daily task.
Thank you for upholding me-
with help each time I ask.

Thank you for the little things-
that made my day so bright.
Thank you for my little child
who hugged me close tonight.

Thank you for that friendly smile-
that someone gave to me.
Thank you for my eyes dear Lord-
so that smile I could see.

Thank Lord for loving me-
and showing that you care -
But best of all I thank you Lord-
for always being there.

I will both lay down in peace and sleep- for you
*Lord only makes me dwell in safety. **Psalm 4:8 KJV***

DAILY PRAYER

Lord help me to worthy- of this day you've given me.
Help me use it wisely- so your glory all will see.

This special day in my life-will not return again-
Help me use it serving you-and not with selfish sin.

Each moment-oh how precious-to use it as I will-
Help your humble servant-each day with goodness fill.

The path of the just is a shining light that shines more
and more into a perfect day. ***Proverbs 4:18 NKJV***

WEDDING PRAYER

As newlyweds we ask of you as we join hand in hand-
You'll not forget to pray that we-honor our wedding band.

They were placed upon our fingers-as a symbol of our love-
Pray God will grant us happiness and blessings from above.

Even though trials do come- and come they surely will-
Again we ask that you will pray- in our lives we may fulfill-

The love that God gave to us -to share with all our heart-
And keep us in His tender care-til we in death do part.

Let the beauty of the Lord Our God be
*upon us. **Psalms 90:17a KJV***

A CHILDS PRAYER

I'm not so very big, you know-I'm just a child you see-
Can you see me praying Lord- so far away from me?

I'm thanking you for lots of things- for Mom and Dad-so much
For my puppy waiting here for me-close enough to touch.

I've been a little naughty too-I spilled at supper time-
I pinched the cat and broke my trike- but God-did you mind?

Forgive me for my naughtiness-I'm sure it must be sin-
Tomorrow I'll be better, God- for Jesus sake-Amen

Even a child is know by his doings- whether his work is
pure and whether it is right. **Proverbs 20:11 KJV**

A MOTHER'S PRAYER

Keep me ever faithful Lord -in my daily walk with thee.
Keep your presence always near- stay ever close to me.

Keep me ever faithful Lord- when trials are hard to bear-
May each one make me stronger-not burdened down with care.

Keep me ever faithful Lord-as a Mother and a wife-
Give me patience for each one-as I guide each precious life.

Keep me ever faithful Lord-so I can do my best-
In all the tasks you've given me-help me stand the test.

Keep me ever faithful Lord-in every thing I do-
When I succeed I'll gladly say, "I did it all for you."

Let my heart be sound in statutes that I be not ashamed.
Psalms 119:80 KJV

KEEP ME SWEET

Dear Lord-
Keep me sweet when trials come-to crowd my busy day.
Keep me ever patient Lord- in things I do and say.

Help me smile though I am sad-to every one I meet-
Let your love shine in my life -to keep me extra sweet.

I have so much to smile about-a sinner saved from sin-
Help me show your saving grace-so keep me sweet-Amen

Create in me a clean heart, O God and renew a right
spirit within me. **Psalm 51:10 NASB**

A PRAYER OF GUIDANCE

Lord take my hand and guide me-
where you would have me go.
And keep my feet upon the path-
as only you can know.
And if today the way is hard-
my strength is almost gone.
Take my hand within your hand-
and lead me safely on.

Show me your ways O Lord-teach me your paths.
Psalms 25:4 NKJV

EARTHLY MISSION

Lord Help me fulfill my mission-
my reason for being on earth.
You sent me here for a purpose-
although I doubt my worth.
Show me Lord what I must do-
give me a clear cut vision.
So I can say that I have been-
fulfilling my earthly mission.

The will of the Lord be done. **Acts 21:14 NKJV**

INSOMNIA

I lie awake- the night seems so long-
I feel the darkness against my face.
The noisey quietness-and empty gong-
as I toss about from place to place.
So alone- awake with awareness-
multiple thoughts engulf 'til day.
Give me the courage to face tomorrow-
refresh my body with sleep I pray.

Hear my prayer, O Lord and let my cry come unto you.
Psalms 102:1 NKJV

THE SINNER AND THE CHILD

Where have you been so long, Lord
I've tried to look for you.
Then a child told me this story
She says she knows it's true!
How you died to save all sinners-
whether grownup or small-
Does that include me Lord-
does all- mean really all?
Most Christians that I know, Lord-
are busy in the church-
They never bothered me Lord-
or went about to search.
Like this little child so faithful-
who in her simple way-
Showed me your great salvation-
so plain that I could say-
Forgive me for my sinning-
Please save my soul I pray-
And make me faithful as this child-
That you sent to me today.

Hear my prayer O God; give ear to the words of
my mouth.   ***Psalms 54:2 NASB***

A PRAYER TO GROW OLD BY

The lines may show upon my face-
for each care has found it's place.
My eyes may not be quite so bright-
so let my smile bring extra light.
My heart no grudge nor hardness bear-
for others burdens I will care
The pace of time I cannot change-
so help me-my life to rearrange-
As the years march by so dutifully
Help me to grow old beautifully.

O God, thou has taught me from my youth; and hither to have
I declared thy wondrous works. Now also when I'm old and gray
headed O God forsake me not. **Psalms 71:17.18a KJV**

JUST A PIECE OF MY MIND

Lord, look at the mess I've got myself in.
I've failed- and opened my big mouth again.
Words spilled out that were unkind-
as I gave someone a piece of my mind.
Since only a piece was all I could spare-
with less and less at each temper flair-
I'm asking you Lord to help me say-
only helpful words in a sensible way.

Pleasant words are as honeycombs. Sweet to the soul
and health to the bones. **Proverbs 16:24 NKJV**

THANKFUL SONGS IN MY HEART

*Thank you Lord for the songs in my heart
that fill my life each day.
With joy that radiates your love-
by things I do and say.
Let me show the ones I meet-
That my songs can be for them-
For Jesus gave these songs to me-
When I gave my heart to Him.*

*O sing unto the Lord a new song, Sing unto the Lord
all the earth. Sing unto the Lord. Bless His name. Show
forth his salvation from day to day.* **Psalms 96:1,2 NKJV**

YOU KNOW ME SO WELL

Lord, you know me so well-
every fault-every secret I keep.
You know the depths of my being-
and when my sorrows are deep.

You know the times I am tempted-
and the times I fail to be strong.
You helped me through those failures-
and showed me where I was wrong.

Today- I'm asking more favor-
to keep me closer to you.
So when trials are heavy again-
I'll know just what I must do.

You shall know the truth-and the truth shall
make you free. ***John 8:32 NASB***

OPEN MY UNDERSTANDING

Darkness captured light and swept it away
taking the perfection and beauty of day.
Death has caused my loved one to be still-
Lord open my understanding to your will.

Threatening clouds have dimmed the skies-
like rain the tears fall from my eyes-
I only know the day seems bleak-
as understanding of your will I seek.

My life, my joys and sorrows too
combined- I lift them up to you-
I often repeat a saddened Why?
not understanding your will-I cry.

May your daily presence be mine I pray-
So I can rejoice though skies are gray-
Speak to my heart and soul until-
I have peace- and understand your will.

Happy is the man who finds wisdom and the man
who gains understanding.   ***Proverbs 3:13 NKJV***